DISCARDS

CUENTO
DE LUZ

This collection of children's books, inspired by real stories, comes from the heart, and as a result of a collaboration between the What Really Matters Foundation, and the publisher Cuento de Luz.

We share the same dreams, the same hopes, and the same philosophy about spreading universal values.

We hope that families, schools, libraries, adults and children all around the world enjoy these books; that they are both inspired and moved by them, and discover, if they do not know it already, what really matters.

María Franco
What Really Matters Foundation
www.loquedeverdadimporta.org

Ana Eulate
Cuento de Luz
www.cuentodeluz.com

Lopez Lomong
Text © 2016 Ana Eulate
Illustrations © 2016 Nívola Uyá
This edition © 2016 Cuento de Luz SL
Calle Claveles, 10 | Urb. Monteclaro | Pozuelo de Alarcón | 28223 | Madrid | Spain
www.cuentodeluz.com
Title in Spanish: Lopez Lomong
English translation by Jon Brokenbrow
ISBN: 978-84-16733-15-6
Printed in PRC by Shanghai Chenxi Printing Co., Ltd. August 2016, print number 1589-2

STONE
PAPER

NO TREES · NO WATER · NO BLEACH

LOPEZ LOMONG

"We're all destined to use our talent to change people's lives."

Lopez Lomong

Ana Eulate

Illustrated by **Nívola Uyá**

Little Simon picked up the drawing he had just finished. He looked at it with a gleaming smile. The day before, the man who had arrived like an angel, with good news, drawing books and colored pencils, had brought a group of children together around the fire. The moon lit up the night, as well as the hope in the hearts of the children who listened spellbound to the tale of the man "with helping hands." It was a story that was incredible, but quite real: a story which as they listened made them cry tears of joy, and clap their hands in excitement.

It was the story of a little boy just like Simon, who had been born in a village just like his, called Kimotong, in the south of Sudan. For the first six years of his life he lived with his family, helping his father, Awey Lomong, with the cattle, and his mother, Rita Namana, with her daily chores, and running everywhere on his gazelle-like legs. That was why he was known as "Lopepe" which in the Buya language means *fast.*

One Sunday in summer, everything changed. Lopepe was together with his parents at a religious ceremony beneath a great tree when suddenly a group of rebel soldiers arrived making a terrible noise. Lopepe felt the arm of what he thought was a **giant** grab onto him and pull him out of his mother's lap. He was taken away with lots of other children in an army truck, along lost back roads, as lost as the kids were. With his eyes full of tears, and being thrown around because of the potholes in the road, he felt that his childhood had been left behind forever in his village, in Kimotong.

The soldiers locked all of the children up in a shack. They were crowded together, hungry, and the nights were cold. Lopepe, the fast little boy, dreamed of returning home to his family.

One night, there was a glimmer of light in the darkness. He met three boys who were older than him, who would protect him and become his **three angels**. They promised him that he would see his mother again. They had been there for three weeks, and they planned to run away. Lopepe would go with them, but they warned him that he would have to run and run, as if he were being swept along by the wind. Run without looking back, run without rest.

And that is what they did. The four of them escaped without being seen through a hole in the wire fence. They ran and ran like gazelles across the savannah, barefoot, for three days.

The reached the frontier with Kenya, and were taken to a United Nations refugee camp in a place called Kakuma.

There Lopepe's life revolved around his new family of eleven little boys who were lost just like him. They shared a tent together, and what little food there was. He never heard from his three angels again. His three friends who had run away with him had vanished.

Lopepe loved playing soccer, although in Kakuma it was more a way of life than a game. It also helped to take his mind off his empty stomach, and not think about food constantly.

More and more refugees arrived. The camp was enormous. Everyday Lopepe ran eighteen miles, the distance around the perimeter of the camp, while he waited for his turn to play soccer. Although it was terribly hot and he was very thirsty, running made him feel free and connected to his mother, who was far away, but beneath the same great sky.

The thing that really opened Lopepe's eyes and remained etched in his memory forever, was the day that he and some of the other children from Kakuma sneaked away to a farmer's home to watch their first Olympic Games on a small black and white television connected to a battery. They were the 2000 games in Sydney, Australia, and the runner Michael Johnson was about to change his life forever. As Lopepe watched him step up onto the podium to receive his medal with tears of joy in his eyes, he knew that one day he too would be an Olympic athlete.

That night, as he walked back to the camp alone beneath the starry sky, he was certain of what his future would hold.

The church in the refugee camp was an oasis: a window on a wider world that Lopepe visited every Sunday. It was very important in his life. It was a special place where he was baptized, confirmed, and took communion on Christmas Eve.

One Sunday in October, the priest of the church in the camp told them some amazing news. They would choose some children who could build a new life with foster families in the United States of America. To be chosen, they would have to write an essay in English. Lopepe wrote his life, and poured all of his heart and soul into the words. His friends helped him to translate it from Swahili into English.

He knew that another life awaited him there, far beyond the fence of Kakuma, a life much, much farther away.

Syracuse

New York

Welcome!

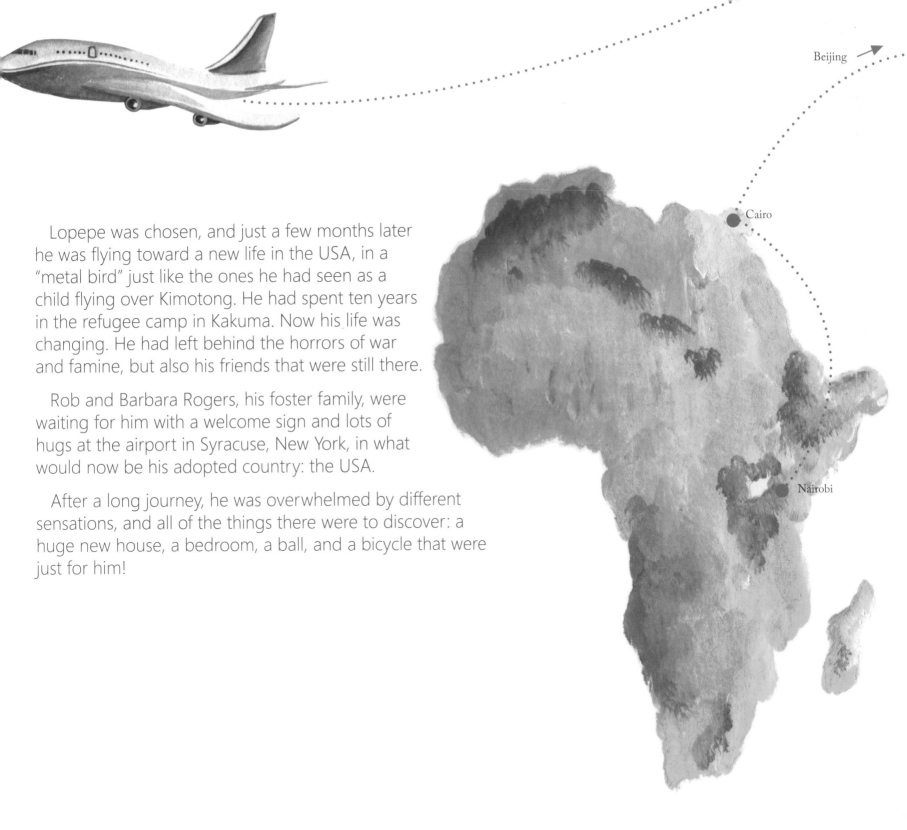

Lopepe was chosen, and just a few months later he was flying toward a new life in the USA, in a "metal bird" just like the ones he had seen as a child flying over Kimotong. He had spent ten years in the refugee camp in Kakuma. Now his life was changing. He had left behind the horrors of war and famine, but also his friends that were still there.

Rob and Barbara Rogers, his foster family, were waiting for him with a welcome sign and lots of hugs at the airport in Syracuse, New York, in what would now be his adopted country: the USA.

After a long journey, he was overwhelmed by different sensations, and all of the things there were to discover: a huge new house, a bedroom, a ball, and a bicycle that were just for him!

Beijing

Cairo

Nairobi

The first night, Lopepe slept with the light on. He didn't know that you could turn off something that lit you up like the sun just by flicking the switch!

His next discovery was the shower the following morning. The water was so cold, and so hot! He soon learned to adjust the temperature, but he wondered if his skin would turn white from washing it so much!

Shortly after arriving in Syracuse, people started to call him Lopez.

Everything was so wonderful he thought there must have been some kind of mistake. He gradually stopped feeling like a lost boy, and started feeling being taken care off.

Jim Paccia came into his life just a few days later. He was the trainer of the cross-country running team at Tully High School, and he tried to convince Lopez to join the team. He showed him a T-shirt with his surname written on the back: LOMONG. It wasn't an easy decision. Lopez wanted to play soccer, not to run, but that T-shirt, with his name on the back was too much to resist.

So he accepted! Tom Carracci, the captain of the cross-country team, would soon become his best friend.

One autumn day, four months after he had arrived, he was on a boat trip with his foster parents on the lake near their home. There he discovered the colors of autumn: the red and yellow of the leaves on the trees. There were no seasons in Kakuma; everything was very dry, and there were dust storms. Rob Rogers stopped the motor in the middle of the lake, and suddenly Lopez felt a great wave of peace flood over him as he opened his heart to them. For the first time, he told them about his past, about his life in the refugee camp, and how sad and lonely he had felt. He discovered how much his adoptive family loved him, and how they were giving him back his lost childhood.

The Rogers then decided to renovate their house to be able to adopt another lost boy. The first to arrive was Dominic, Peter, and later on, Alex.

Shortly afterward, something really amazing and quite unexpected happened. Lopez found out that his biological mother Rita was living in Kenya, and that she had gone to look for him in Kakuma. He was able to find her telephone number, and with his heart thumping like a drum, he called her. When he heard the sound of her voice after so many years, he was overcome by emotion, and tears rolled down his cheeks. They were both alive! They had found each other!

They arranged to see each other as soon as they could. They were a long way apart, and Lopez was going away to study at the University of Norfolk, and then to Northern Arizona University, which was more specialized in athletics.

The road toward his dream of being an elite athlete was becoming more and more clearly defined. Lopez left his footprints on that path the day he won his first 1500 meter race.

Lopez was overcome with joy when he became an American citizen, and shortly after when he was invited to Kenya to meet up once again with his biological mother Rita. It was a hugely emotional moment, which she celebrated by dancing and sprinkling him with fermented flour. Later, together with his parents, he visited his village, Kimotong, where everyone was waiting to celebrate the fact that the little boy they thought was dead had come back to life.

Lopez returned to the USA with his heart overflowing with emotion, and a ring made of green, yellow and black beads that his mother had given to him. It was the ring he would proudly wear when he was the flag bearer for the US Team at the Beijing Olympics, where he was competing as an athlete.

As he proudly held the flag, he thought about all the different experiences he had had: the decision to leave university to become a professional athlete; the effort, the discipline, the courage, the injuries, and the smile of Britanny, the love of his life.

Three years later, the little boy who had once written in the dirt of Kakuma with a stick graduated from the Northern Arizona University, with all of the emotion that comes with feeling and knowing **what really matters**, and that you strive for something with all of your heart, nothing can stand in the way of your dreams.

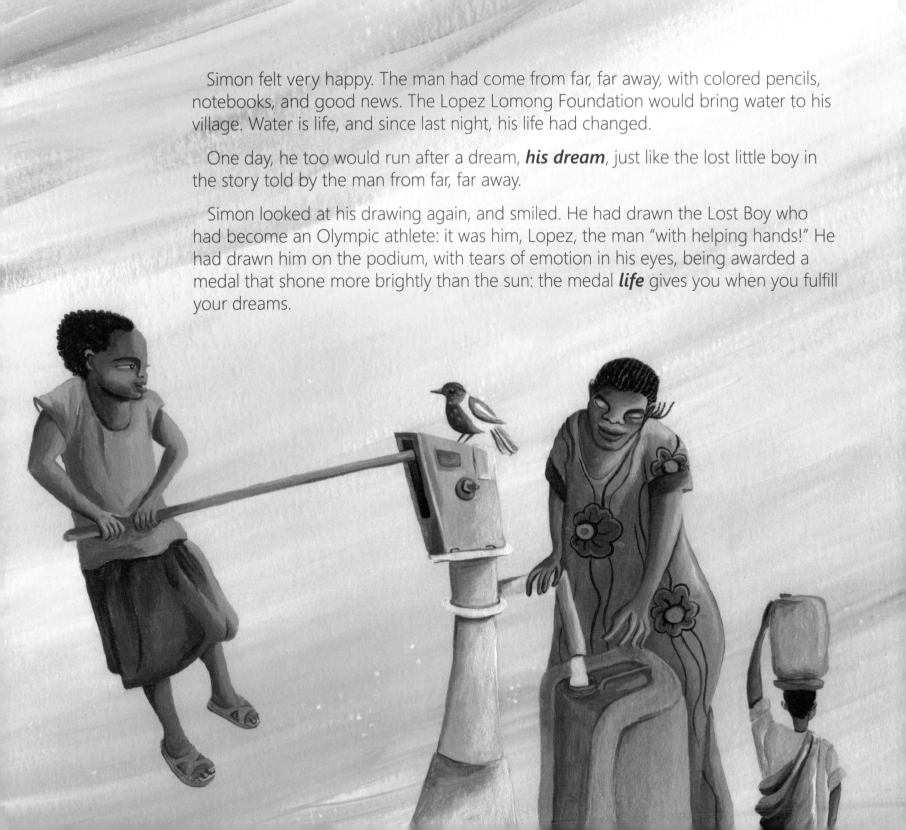

Simon felt very happy. The man had come from far, far away, with colored pencils, notebooks, and good news. The Lopez Lomong Foundation would bring water to his village. Water is life, and since last night, his life had changed.

One day, he too would run after a dream, **his dream**, just like the lost little boy in the story told by the man from far, far away.

Simon looked at his drawing again, and smiled. He had drawn the Lost Boy who had become an Olympic athlete: it was him, Lopez, the man "with helping hands!" He had drawn him on the podium, with tears of emotion in his eyes, being awarded a medal that shone more brightly than the sun: the medal **life** gives you when you fulfill your dreams.

About the *What Really Matters Foundation*

The aim of the What Really Matters Foundation is to promote universal values in society. Its main project consists of the What Really Matters conferences, which are aimed at young people.

Every year, they are held in eight cities in Spain, and in another six countries. During the conferences, a series of speakers share the real and inspiring stories of their lives, which invite us to discover the things that are really important in life. Like the story in the book you're holding in your hands.

You can join us, hear more stories, and find out a little more about us at www.loquedeverdadimporta.org.

We look forward to your visit!

María Franco
What Really Matters Foundation